Best Friends Forever

Best Friends Forever

MQP

The greatest sweetener of human life is friendship. To raise this to the highest pitch of enjoyment, is a secret which but few discover.

Joseph Addison

Two are better than one; because they have a good reward for their labor. For if they fall, the one will lift up his fellow: but woe to him that is alone when he falleth; for he hath not another to help him up.

The Bible, Ecclesiastes 4:9

The ornament of a
house is the friends
who frequent it.

Ralph Waldo Emerson

To like and dislike the same things, that is indeed true friendship.

Sallust

Three little maids who, all unwary,
Come from a ladies' seminary,
Freed from its genius tutelary—
Three little maids from school!
Three little maids from school!

W. S. Gilbert

If a man does not make new acquaintances as he advances through life, he will soon find himself left alone. A man, sir, should keep his friendship in a constant repair.

Samuel Johnson

The most I can do for
my friend is simply to
be his friend. I have no
wealth to bestow on him.
If he knows that I am happy
in loving him, he will want
no other reward. Is not
friendship divine in this?

Henry David Thoreau

Grief can take care of itself, but to get the full value of a joy you must have somebody to divide it with.

Mark Twain

An agreeable companion
on a journey is as good
as a carriage.

Syrus

When friends are at your hearthside met,
Sweet courtesy has done its most
If you have made each guest forget
That he himself is not the host.

Thomas Bailey Aldrich

One who finds a
friend finds a treasure.

Italian proverb

Friendship is always
a sweet responsibility,
never an opportunity.

Kahlil Gibran

Whosoever loveth me
loveth my hound.

Sir Thomas More

We are easily consoled
for the misfortunes of
our friends if they give
us the chance to prove
our devotion.

François, duc de La Rochefoucauld

My friends are
my estate.

Emily Dickinson

If two friends ask you to judge a dispute, don't accept, because you will lose one friend; on the other hand, if two strangers come with the same request, accept because you will gain one friend.

Saint Augustine

The language of
friendship is not
words but meanings.

Henry David Thoreau

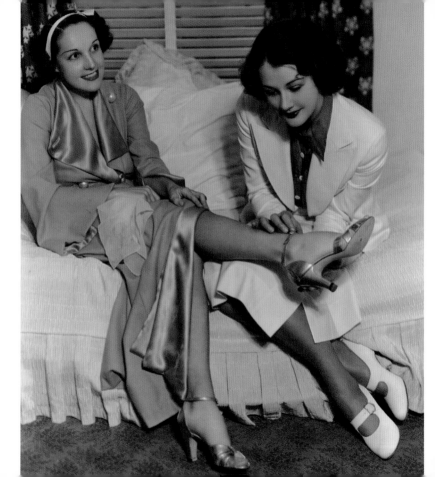

With clothes the new
are best; with friends
the old are best.

Chinese proverb

There is magic in the memory of schoolboy friendships; it softens the heart, and even affects the nervous system of those who have no heart.

Benjamin Disraeli

It is not so much our friends'
help that helps us as the
confident knowledge that
they will help us.

Epicurus

43

The dog was created specially for children. He is the god of frolic.

Henry Ward Beecher

It is one of the blessings of
old friends that you can
afford to be stupid with them.

Ralph Waldo Emerson

We are all travelers in
the wilderness of this
world, and the best that
we find in our travels is
an honest friend.

Robert Louis Stevenson

49

Well;
I am not of that feather to shake off
My friend when he must need me.

William Shakespeare

The best mirror is
an old friend.

George Herbert

Love is only chatter,
Friends are all that matter.

Gelett Burgess

Two friends, two
bodies with one
soul inspir'd.

Homer

Friendship is the only cement that will hold the world together.

Woodrow Wilson

Somehow we manage it: to like our friends,
   to tolerate not only their little ways
but their huge neuroses, their monumental
   oddness:
"Oh well," we smile, "it's one of his funny days."

Fleur Adcock

Thus nature has no love for solitude, and always leans, as it were, on some support; and the sweetest support is found in the most intimate friendship.

Cicero

A true friend is the greatest of all blessings, and that which we take the least care of all to acquire.

François, duc de La Rochefoucauld

Friendship is one
mind in two bodies.

Mencius

The greatest pleasure of a dog is that you may make a fool of yourself with him, and not only will he not scold you, but he will make a fool of himself, too.

Samuel Butler

We have been friends together
In sunshine and in shade.

Caroline Norton

71

Cameras are so simple to operate now that taking pictures is much easier than getting friends to look at them.

Hugh Allen

The bird a nest
the spider a web
man friendship.

William Blake

The glory of friendship is not the outstretched hand, nor the kindly smile, nor the joy of companionship; it is the spiritual inspiration that comes to one when he discovers that someone else believes in him and is willing to trust him.

Ralph Waldo Emerson

Friendship is a sheltering tree.

Samuel Taylor Coleridge

Don't walk in front of me,
I may not follow.
Don't walk behind me,
I may not lead. Walk
beside me and be my friend.

Albert Camus

A friend may well
be reckoned the
masterpiece of nature.

Ralph Waldo Emerson

One can never speak enough
of the virtues, the dangers,
the power of shared laughter.

Françoise Sagan

Then come, my friend, forget your
    foes, and leave your fears behind,
And wander forth to try your luck,
    with cheerful, quiet mind.

Henry Jackson van Dyke

"Esther, it's enough to make anybody but me jealous," said Caddy, laughing and shaking her head; "but it only makes me joyful, for you are the first friend I ever had, and the best friend I ever can have, and nobody can respect and love you too much to please me."

Charles Dickens

There is nothing so great that I fear to do it for my friend; nothing so small that I will disdain to do it for him.

Sir Philip Sidney

What joy is better than news of friends?

Robert Browning

The proper office of a friend is to side with you when you are in the wrong. Nearly anybody will side with you when you are in the right.

Mark Twain

It is a sweet thing,
friendship, a dear balm,
A happy and auspicious
bird of calm....

Percy Bysshe Shelley

I keep my friends as misers
do their treasure, because,
of all the things granted us
by wisdom, none is greater
or better than friendship.

Pietro Aretino

Nothing makes the earth seem so spacious as to have friends at a distance: they make the latitudes and longitudes.

Henry David Thoreau

Hold a true friend
with both your hands.

Nigerian proverb

Each friend represents
a world in us, a world
possibly not born until
they arrive, and it is only
by this meeting that a
new world is born.

Anaïs Nin

Treat people as if they were what they ought to be, and you help them to become what they are capable of being.

Johann Wolfgang von Goethe

My best friend is the one who brings out the best in me.

Henry Ford

Picture Credits

Cover: Peekaboo, 1953. p.5: Tennis Interval, 1934. p.6: Bumps A Daisy, 1933. p.9: Singalong, 1949. p.11: Lots Of Puff, 1935. p.12: Sleeping Beauties, 1953. p.15: Grandfathers, 1949. p.17: Tree Children, circa 1955. p.18: Glass Catch, circa 1935. p.21: Pedalo Boat, 1947. p.22: A Few Friends Round, circa 1955, © Lambert/Getty Images. p.25: Little Lamb, 1934. p.27: Candy Floss, 1953. p.28: Worried Friend, 1935. p.31: Good Friend, circa 1945, © Lambert/Getty Images. p.32: Day Trippers, 1935. p.35: Board Game Fun, circa 1956. p.37: Barbara's Friend, 1954. p.38: Lovely New Shoes, circa 1935. p.41: Playground Friends, circa 1953. p.42: Copycat, 1952. p.45: Canine Friends, circa 1955. p.46: Hairwash, 1955. p.48: Pavement Riders, 1936. p.51: Parrot Pal, 1941. p.52: Tete-A-Tete, 1956. p.55: Firm Friends, 1939. p.56: Doggy Driver, 1937. p.59: A Young Man's Fancy, 1937. p.60: In Confidence, 1939. p.63: Friends, 1939. p.64: Great Great Friends, 1959. p.67: Holiday Pals, 1949. p.69: Best Friends, 1926. p.70: Fun In The Sun, circa 1955, © Camerique/Getty Images. p.73: Sombreros, circa 1951. p.74: Children Knitting, 1935. p.77: Country Stream, 1954. p.78: As cover. p.80: Out Door Larks, circa 1945. p.83: Penguin Pal, 1937. p.84: Happy Beauties, 1953. p.87: Fishing Friends, circa 1965, © Lambert/Getty Images. p.88: Best Friends, 1974. p.91: Pet Mouse, circa 1955. p.92: Royal Replies, 1936. p.94: Holiday Chat, 1954. p.97: Furry Friend, 1949. p.98: Miniature Dancers, circa 1955. p.101: Schoolgirl Reunion, 1952. p.103: Boating Friends, circa 1945. p.104: Picnic, 1971. p.106: Ballet Class, 1955. p.109: Two Friends, 1954.

Text Credits

p.26: Excerpt from *The Prophet,* by Kahlil Gibran, published by Random House, 2001. p.61: Excerpt from "A Hymn to Friendship" by Fleur Adcock from *Time Zones,* published by Oxford University Press, 1991. p.81: Excerpt by Albert Camus, used by kind permission of Éditions Gallimard. p.105: Excerpt by Anaïs Nin reprinted by kind permission of The Anaïs Nin Trust, c/o Barbara W. Stuhlmann, Author's Representative.

Published by MQ Publications Limited
12 The Ivories, 6–8 Northampton Street, London, N1 2HY
Tel: + 44 (0)20 7359 2244   Fax: + 44 (0)20 7359 1616
e-mail: mail@mqpublications.com
website: www.mqpublications.com

ISBN: 1-84072-478-1

35790864

Text compilation: Wynn Wheldon

Printed and bound in China